W9-CEN-572

DATE DUE

Veterans Day

Mir Tamim Ansary

Heinemann Library
Chicago, Illinois

© 1999 Reed Educational & Professional Publishing
Published by Heinemann Library,
an imprint of Reed Educational & Professional Publishing,
Chicago, IL

Customer Service 888-454-2279
Visit our website at www.heinemannlibrary.com

Printed and bound in Hong Kong

03 02 01
10 9 8 7 6 5 4 3

Library of Congress Cataloging-in-Publication Data
Ansary, Mir Tamim, 1954-
    Veterans Day / Mir Tamim Ansary.
      p.   cm. — (Holiday histories)
    Includes bibliographical references and index.
    Summary: Introduces Veterans Day, explaining the historical events
behind it, how it became a holiday, and how it is observed.
    ISBN 1-57572-876-1 (lib.bdg.)
    1. Veterans Day—Juvenile literature.   [1. Veterans Day.
. Holidays.] I. Title. II. Series: Ansary, Mir Tamim. Holiday
histories.
D671.A75   1998
394.264—dc21   98-14376
                                                            CIP
                                                            AC

Acknowledgments
The publisher would like to thank the following for permission to reproduce photographs:

Cover: Reuters/Corbis-Bettmann

Stock Boston/Bob Daemmrick, p. 4; AP/WideWorld, pp. 6, 7, 13(all), 16, 18(right), 19, 22, 24,
26(right); Corbis-Bettmann/Alexander Alland Sr., p. 8; The Granger Collection, pp. 9, 18(center);
UPI/Corbis-Bettmann, pp. 10, 11, 14; Corbis, p. 12; Super Stock, pp. 15(all), 26(left); Corbis-
Bettmann, pp. 18(left), 23; Corbis-Bettmann/Baldwin H. Ward, p. 20; Reuters/Corbis-Bettmann, p.
27; AP/Wide World, p. 28.

Every effort has been made to contact copyright holders of any material reproduced in this book.
Any omissions will be rectified in subsequent printings if notice is given to the publisher.

Some words are shown in bold, **like this**. You can find
out what they mean by looking in the glossary.

Contents

A Day for Veterans

November 11 is Veterans Day in the United States. A crowd has gathered in the park to watch a parade.

Many people think this is just another day off
from school or work. But Veterans Day
means much more to these people. That is
because they are veterans themselves.

What Is a Veteran?

A veteran is someone who has been in the **armed forces**. Many of these veterans fought in wars. Some fought in the Persian Gulf War in 1991.

Some even fought in World War Two, way back in the 1940s. All these veterans risked their lives for our country.

Before Veterans Day

How did this holiday begin? Let's go back to a time before Veterans Day. Your great grandparents were young then. America was at peace.

But Europe was **tense**. In Europe, many
small countries were ruled by bigger ones.
Millions of angry people wanted to be free.

World War!

Some of the big countries wanted more land.
But their neighbors in other countries did too.
So both sides were building strong armies.

In 1914, a war began. Germany helped one
side. Russia helped the other. Soon, more
than 30 countries were fighting.

America Fights

German submarines started sinking American ships. The United States decided to make war on Germany. In 1917, U.S. **troops** sailed to Europe.

The fighting stopped on November 11 at
11 o'clock, when Germany **surrendered.**
The First World War was over. More than
fourteen million people had died.

★

Armistice Day

In 1919, President Woodrow Wilson called November 11 a holiday. He called it Armistice Day. Armistice means "to stop fighting."

That day, many people wore red poppies.
They did so to remember Flanders Field. A
bloody battle was fought in that poppy field.

★

Honoring Peace

At eleven o'clock that day, many people became quiet. They kept silent for two minutes. This was a way to **honor** the peace.

These **customs** were repeated every year after that. People gave thanks for peace. They honored the soldiers who had won the peace.

German dictator
Adolf Hitler

Italian dictator
Benito Mussolini

Japanese general
Hideki Tojo

Trouble Again

But the peace did not last. Cruel **dictators**
took over Germany and Italy. Powerful
generals took over Japan.

18

These countries teamed up as the Axis Powers. In 1935, they started to attack other countries. They planned to take over the world.

World War Two

The world fought back. In 1939, World War Two began. It was much more deadly than World War One. Armies had more powerful guns now.

The war spread all over the world. There
was fighting in 57 countries. There were
battles on land and at sea. There were battles
in the air.

★

The Axis Powers Fail

In 1941, Japanese airplanes bombed U.S.
ships and planes in Hawaii. After that, the
United States entered the war.

The Axis Powers were **defeated** in 1945.
World War Two ended. More than 50
million people had died in this war.

Celebrating Veterans Today

After the war, Americans were glad to celebrate Armistice Day again. But in 1954, the name was changed to Veterans Day.

Now, on Veterans Day, we celebrate all our veterans. Most of all, we **honor** those who died. We thank them for all that we have. They gave all they had.

★

Our Armed Forces

Today, we have a powerful army, air force, and navy. We have the Marines and the Coast Guard.

We stay ready even when there is no war.
Our forces help keep peace in troubled places.
We hope they can stop another war from
starting.

The Eleventh Hour

The parade is over and the crowds are gone. But one Vietnam War veteran stays. This man loves peace because he has seen war. That is why he stands here on the eleventh day of the eleventh month.

The eleventh hour strikes at last. The veteran bows his head and falls silent. In his silence, he remembers friends who never came back from battle.

★
28

Important Dates

Veterans Day

1914	World War One begins
1914	The Battle of Flanders Field
1917	The United States enters the war
1918	World War One ends
1919	Armistice Day becomes a national holiday
1922	Mussolini takes power in Italy
1926	Army officers take power in Japan
1933	Hitler takes power in Germany
1935	Italy invades Abyssinia
1939	World War Two begins
1941	Japan bombs U.S. ships at Pearl Harbor
1945	World War Two ends
1954	Armistice Day is changed to Veterans Day

Glossary

armed forces   country's army, air force, and navy

customs   things people always do on special days or for certain events

defeated   to lose

dictators   leaders who use force to govern

Europe   one of the seven continents

honor   to show respect for something

surrendered   gave up

tense   full of worry

troops   soldiers

More Books to Read

Granfield, Linda. *In Flanders Field: The story of the Poem by John McCrae.* New York: Bantam Doubleday Dell, 1996.

Sorenson, Lynda. *Veterans Day.* Vero Beach, Fla: Rourk Press, 1994.

Spies, Karen. *Our National Holidays.* Brookfield, Conn: Millbrook Press, 1992.

Index